World of Faiths

Christianity

Alan Brown

QED Publishing

A catalogue record for this book is available from the British Library.

ISBN 978 1 84538 706 8

Written by Alan Brown
Designed by Tall Tree Books
Editor Louisa Somerville
Consultant John Keast

Publisher Steve Evans
Creative Director Zeta Davies
Editorial Director Jean Coppendale

Printed and bound in China

Picture credits
Key: t = top, b = bottom, c = centre, l = left, r = right, FC = front cover

Ark Religion/Helen Rogers title page, 4, 6, 7t, 7b, 8, 9t, 10t, 10b, 12, 13, 18, 19t, 19b, 20, 21t, 21c, 22 /Bob Turner 5t,
23b /Archie Miles 11cl /Ken Mclaren 16 /Chris Rennie 17t /Vladimir Sidoropolev 17b /George Wittenberg 23t
/Adina Tovy 24 /Mark Both 25c /Hanan Isachar 25t, 27t; **Corbis**/Hulton-Deutsch Collection 21b /Sygma 26.

Website information is correct at the time of going to press.
However, the publishers cannot accept liability for any
information or links found on third-party websites.

Words in **bold** are explained
in the glossary on page 30.

Contents

What is a Christian?

A Christian is someone who follows the teachings of Jesus Christ, who lived 2,000 years ago. He was a preacher and teacher who lived in Palestine (most of which is in present-day Israel). At the age of about 36, Jesus was arrested and **crucified** on a cross. In the centuries after his death, his followers spread his teachings far and wide.

▼ Children attend their First Communion in a Roman Catholic church (see page 23).

What do Christians believe?

Christians believe that Jesus is God's only son. They believe that Jesus was born on Earth so that people could be saved from **sin**. In the Christian holy book, the Bible, it says that three days after he was crucified, Jesus rose from the dead and returned to heaven to be with God. For Christians, Jesus' life shows that those who are saved will join God in heaven after their death.

Going to church

A church is a building where Christians **worship**. Christians come together here to sing hymns of praise to God, to confess (admit) their sins and to pray. Many Christians go to church on Sunday, but some Christians never attend church.

▶ St. Peter's Cathedral in Rome, Italy, is the focus for all Roman Catholics (see page 16-17).

Christian symbols

There are many signs of Christianity all around the world, from a 'Jesus saves' sticker in the rear window of a car to a grand **cathedral** in a capital city. Christians sometimes wear a cross or fish symbol (see page 9) around their neck. In the Bible, Jesus describes himself as 'Alpha and Omega', meaning first and last. So, Christians may also wear these symbols.

Alpha and Omega symbols

Fish symbol

Christianity worldwide

As Christianity has spread around the world, different countries have developed their own Christian customs. In Mexico, on the Day of the Dead (November 2nd) Mexicans remember their dead by decorating graves with flowers and offerings of food, such as skull-shaped sweets.

Who was Jesus?

Jesus was born in Bethlehem, which is in present-day Israel, around 6BCE. At that time the land was ruled by the Romans. Later, he moved with his mother, Mary, and his father, Joseph, to Nazareth in northern Israel. Here he grew up among his own people, the Jews.

Jesus the teacher

Jesus travelled around Palestine with his 12 **disciples**. He taught people that they should believe in and obey God, love themselves and one another. He taught that God loved them and would forgive them their sins. Thousands of people flocked to hear Jesus preach. The Bible says he also performed **miracles**, such as healing the sick and giving life to dead people.

▲ Mary's special relationship with her son, Jesus, makes her important to many Christians.

Arrest and death

Because he said he was the Son of God, the religious leaders of the Jews accused Jesus of **blasphemy**. Jesus was arrested and handed over to Pontius Pilate, the Roman governor, who tried him and had him crucified. His disciples took him down from the cross and placed his body in a tomb. It says in the Bible that three days later, Jesus came back from the dead. He met his followers, talked and ate with them. Finally, he was taken into heaven to be with God, his Father.

▶ Crucifixion on a cross was the way the Romans killed criminals, as a warning to others not to break Roman law.

◀ Christians believe that three days after he was crucified, Jesus Christ rose from the dead and walked out of his tomb.

Jesus lives

Jesus promised his disciples that he would not leave them. The disciples taught others that Jesus was always beside them. Christians still believe in God the Holy Spirit, which is God's power in people's lives. They worship God in three forms, the Trinity – God the Father, God the Son (Jesus) and God the Holy Spirit.

7

How did Christianity spread?

After Jesus' death, his disciples were frightened to think what might happen next. At the Jewish festival of Pentecost, they were all together in a room when they felt wind rushing past them. In the Bible, it says that tongues of fire touched each disciple, filling them with the Holy Spirit. They took this to be a sign that God was with them, just as Jesus had promised. It gave them the courage to spread the good news of Jesus' teachings.

Peter the Rock

Simon, one of Jesus' disciples, was given a new name by Jesus – Peter, meaning 'rock'. Peter was the rock on which the Christian Church would be built. Peter wanted Jesus' message to be heard far and wide. He and Paul (see opposite) became the main leaders of the Christians. The new religion spread to North Africa and beyond. Peter went to Rome, where he became the first head, or patriarch, of the Church. He was later made a saint.

▶ Peter is often pictured holding a key because Jesus told him he would have the keys of the Kingdom of Heaven.

Saul becomes Paul

A man called Saul of Tarsus **persecuted** the early Christians. One day, he was on his way to Damascus when he had a vision of Jesus asking why he was being cruel to Christians. Saul was stunned. He realized that he didn't have an answer. Afterwards he changed his name to Paul, to show that he was a 'new' person. He became a well-known Christian teacher, travelling around the Mediterranean, and writing many letters that are now in the Bible.

◀ Paul holds the sword of truth, to show that he teaches the truth about Jesus.

The fish

To avoid persecution, early Christians would draw a fish as a secret symbol to show one another that they believed in Jesus. The Greek word for fish was 'ichthus'. In Greek, the letters stand for: 'Jesus Christ, God's Son, Saviour'.

Make a fish symbol mobile

You will need: thin card • ruler • pencil • a pair of compasses • black felt-tip pen • scissors • string • 2 metal coat hangers • cotton thread

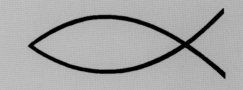

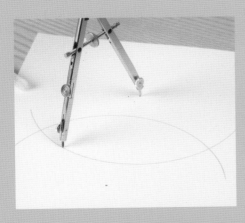

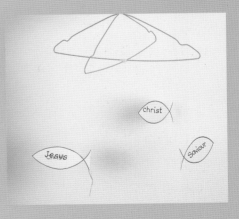

1 On card, make two pencil marks 12cm apart. Using the marks to position your compass, draw two arcs that cross each other. Using the lines as a guide, draw a fish in felt-tip pen.

2 Cut around the fish, just outside the black lines. Make four more fish. Write one of these words on each one: Jesus, Christ, God's, Son, Saviour. Make a hole in each fish with a sharp pencil.

3 Tie the coat hangers together at right angles and feed thread onto each fish. Hang one fish from each corner of your mobile and one from the centre where the hangers cross.

9

The Bible

▲ This is a very old copy of the New Testament of the Bible, which was originally written in Greek. The Old Testament was written in Hebrew, the language of the Jews.

The Bible is the Christians' holy book. It is divided into two sections, the Old and New Testaments. They both record the relationship between God and humankind over hundreds of years. The word testament means 'promise', and Christians believe that the Bible reveals the story of God's plan for the world and His promises to all people.

▲ Knowledge of the Bible is important to all Christians. This family is reading the stories of God's action and the events of Jesus' life.

The Old Testament

The Old Testament (or Promise) describes the time from the **Creation** to just before the birth of Jesus. It tells of God's promise to Abraham and his descendants, the Jewish people, that if they obeyed him he would always love and protect them. It includes many well-known stories, such as Adam and Eve, Noah's Ark and David and Goliath. Christians believe that the Old Testament also tells of the coming of their Saviour, Jesus.

The New Testament

The New Testament is about Jesus being sent into the world by God, to offer forgiveness and new life to those who believe in him. It includes the Gospels (or books) of Matthew, Mark, Luke and John. Each disciple describes Jesus' life, death and **resurrection** from their point of view. The New Testament also tells the story of how the Christian church started and how the disciples spread the teachings of Jesus. The last book contains predictions for the future of the world. The New Testament was written in Greek, probably between 50CE and 110CE.

The Bible translated

By 100CE, the Old Testament had been translated from Hebrew into Greek. Later, by about 390CE, both of the testaments were translated into Latin. The first Bible in English was published in 1535. Today, it is available in every known written language.

Make a decorated letter

You will need: sheet of white paper • pencil • pencil crayons • felt-tip pens or paint • gold metallic pen

In medieval times, when Bibles were handwritten by monks, they often decorated the first letter on a page with beautiful patterns and pictures.

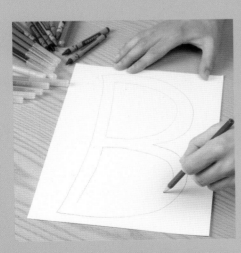

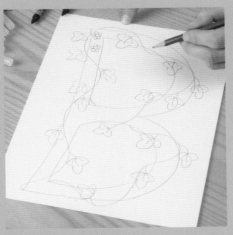

1 Using a pencil, draw a solid capital letter on the paper. Make it as big as possible to fill as much of the paper as you can.

2 Draw a vine curling around your letter. Add leaves growing on the vine. Then draw on small flowers, or your own design.

3 Colour in the letter with coloured crayon. Use felt-tip pens for the vine and flowers. Draw on a border with gold pen.

What did Jesus teach?

Jesus spread his message by preaching to people, by telling parables (stories) and by the example of how he lived his own life. In the Bible it also says that he performed miracles.

Parables

A parable is a story with a message. Jesus used parables to help people understand his religious message. He based them on everyday life, so that the things he talked about were familiar to his listeners. A parable can be enjoyed as a good story but also teaches people how to behave in a Christian way.

The Lost Sheep

Jesus told a parable about a shepherd who had lost one of his 100 sheep. He went searching for the sheep, found it and brought it back to the sheep pen. In Jesus' time, a shepherd with 100 sheep was a rich person. When Jesus told this story, some listeners laughed. Why, they asked, would such a wealthy man bother to look for one sheep? Jesus told the story to show the love God has for everyone and how he looks for each one who goes astray – just like the shepherd searching for his one lost sheep.

▼ The shepherd saves his sheep. Christians believe that Jesus saves them, too.

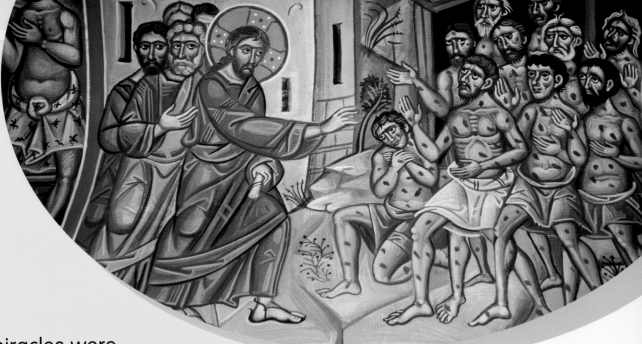

▶ Jesus heals ten men with **leprosy**. They are overjoyed – but only one says 'Thank you'.

Miracles

Traditionally, miracles were believed to be signs of God's power. The Bible describes Jesus performing miracles, such as calming a storm when his disciples were afraid and healing a paralyzed man by telling him his sins were forgiven. Jesus wanted to show God's power in action. There have been many healers before, during and since Jesus' time. Today, many Christians claim to have Jesus' power to heal.

'A man came to Jesus with leprosy. He fell on his face before Jesus and said, "If you will, Lord, you can heal me." Jesus stretched out his hand and touched him saying, "I will: be clean." Immediately the man's leprosy disappeared.'
Luke 5.12-15

The Paralyzed Man

Some men brought a paralyzed man to Jesus but when they came to the house where he was teaching, they could not get in because of the crowd. They dug a hole through the roof and let the paralyzed man down on a stretcher into the crowd. Jesus said, "Your sins are forgiven. Take up your bed and walk." And the man did so. People thought that illness was caused by sinning. If your sins were forgiven, you could be cured.

13

The Sermon on the Mount

Jesus had been travelling all over Galilee. Huge crowds of people turned up to listen to him speak as word spread that he could heal sickness and disease. One day, the crowd was so huge that Jesus climbed up to the top of a mountain, so that everyone could see and hear him talk. The **sermon** that he gave that day became known as the Sermon on the Mount. It was based on his teachings found in the Gospels of the Bible.

Jesus' message

Jesus wanted people to understand that helping others would make their own lives better. Jesus told them to love their enemies, not to judge other people and to be prepared to forgive them. Jesus was very concerned for the poor and for the **outcasts** in society. He asked all the listeners in the crowd to remember to put other people's needs first.

Jesus' teaching on wealth

Jesus told the crowd that it was very difficult for a wealthy person to go to heaven because having a lot of money can make a person selfish. He said, "It is easier for a camel to go through the eye of a needle than for a rich man to enter the Kingdom of Heaven." Jesus told the crowd not to worry about practical things, such as having clothes to wear and enough food to eat. "Put your trust and faith in God," he said, "and everything will be provided for you."

Christianity around the world

Christianity has spread all over the world. Christians in different places have developed their own styles of worship. There are about 23,000 Christian **sects** worldwide today, including millions of Methodists and Baptists. There are about 70 million **Anglicans**, but half the Christians in the world are Roman Catholic.

▼ In the 1500s, Spanish invaders brought the Roman Catholic faith to South America. Here, a holy procession is taking place through the streets of Cusco, Peru.

The Church divided

After Jesus' death, his followers became more organized over time. About 1,000 years ago, the **Pope** in Rome, Italy, and the Patriarch of Constantinople (now Istanbul), Turkey, were the two most powerful Christian leaders. The Pope claimed to be the leader of all Christians but the Patriarch did not agree. The Church split, and the Patriarch became leader of the Orthodox Church in Constantinople.

Protestants

As time went on, some Catholics felt that the Roman Catholic Church was no longer following Jesus' teaching and was too rich and powerful. About 500 years ago, some people began to protest against the Church's teaching. These people and their followers became known as Protestants.

▶ A group of Japanese Christians sing about their faith at an open-air service. They belong to a group of Protestants called **Evangelicals**.

▲ A priest uses sweet-smelling smoke, called incense, to bless the worshippers. He swings a censer (a golden bowl on chains) back and forth.

More division

The Protestants believed that Christians should look to the Bible and God's Holy Spirit for guidance, not to the Pope. The Protestants split from the Roman Catholic Church. Over the next few hundred years, the Protestant Church split again into further groups, including the Methodists, Evangelicals, Baptists and Anglicans. They all follow Jesus' teachings, but in different ways.

The Church reunited?

Today, there are thousands of Christian groups, or Churches, around the world. The ecumenical movement reminds Christians that although they may worship differently, they all share a belief in Jesus and his teachings. Most churches are members of this movement.

How do Christians worship?

Christians worship as individuals and in groups. They may worship privately, saying their prayers to God and reading the Bible. They also come together in churches to praise God and confess their sins. Traditionally, churches were built in the form of a cross, with the **altar** at the east end so that it faced Jerusalem, Israel.

Orthodox churches

In every Orthodox church, there is a screen called the iconostasis. It separates the people from the holiest part of the church, called the sanctuary, where the altar stands. The priests move in front of and behind the iconostasis through a pair of doors, which are often beautifully decorated.

◀ The iconostasis doors may be covered with small paintings of Jesus, Mary or the saints, called icons.

Roman Catholic churches

In Roman Catholic churches the altar is very important as the main service of worship, called Mass, is celebrated there. All Catholic churches also have a wooden box or screen, called the confessional screen. People confess their sins to the priest, who sits on the other side of the screen.

▲ Christians can pray anywhere. They shut out the world to talk to God.

Inside a church

Some churches are decorated with statues, paintings of Jesus and stained-glass windows illustrating Bible stories. Others have no decoration at all.
In most churches, there is a pulpit, a font where new Christians are baptized, a stand for the Bible called a lectern and pews where the congregation sits.

Protestant churches

Protestant churches are often plainer than Orthodox churches. The altar is a simple table in memory of Jesus' **Last Supper**. Preaching forms a main part of Protestant worship so the pulpit, where the priest stands to give his sermons (talks), is important.

▲ The oldest Protestant church in Amsterdam, Netherlands. It has hardly any decoration.

19

Holy people

Most churches have one special person to lead the services and care for the congregation. Church leaders include bishops, priests, ministers and pastors. Some are well known throughout the world. Other holy people such as **monks** and **nuns** might live in religious communities.

The pope and bishops

The Catholic church is led by the Pope, whom Catholics believe is the direct successor of the disciple Peter, the first pope (see page 8). Below him in authority are the bishops and below them the parish priests. The Anglican and Orthodox Churches also have priests and bishops, but only the Anglican Church allows women to become priests.

◀ A Roman Catholic bishop holds up the **wafer** at a Mass. The wafer **symbolizes** the bread that Jesus ate at the Last Supper.

Ministers and pastors

Some Churches do not have priests. They call their leaders, of both sexes, ministers or pastors. It is the job of the leaders to serve the members of the Church and look after them, rather like a shepherd caring for his flock. Ministers and pastors are usually chosen and elected by the church community.

▶ Many Scout and Guide groups are associated with churches, where they learn about the message of God.

Mother Teresa (1910-1997)

Mother Teresa was a nun who worked among poor people in Calcutta, India, and elsewhere, regardless of their religion. She was awarded the **Nobel Peace Prize** for her work.

Martin Luther King (1929-1968)

A Baptist minister, called Martin Luther King was a powerful speaker who wanted equality for black people in the USA and was awarded the Nobel Peace Prize. He was shot dead for his views.

The Polish pope

Pope John Paul II was the first Polish pope and the youngest ever to be elected. He died in 2005. Pope John Paul II travelled the world, visiting many more countries than any other pope. He was well known and popular. Soon after his death, the Roman Catholic Church started the process of making him a saint.

Family celebrations

Christians think of themselves as members of a church family. They celebrate important events in their lives with the family of other worshippers at church. The Roman Catholic, Orthodox and Protestant Churches all celebrate events such as weddings in different ways.

Baptism

Jesus was **baptized** by his cousin John before he began teaching. Many Christians are baptized after birth, too. Parents and godparents promise to teach the child about Christianity, and candles are lit to symbolize how Jesus brought light into the world.

▼ The priest pours holy water over the baby's head and marks it with the sign of the cross.

◀ Roman Catholic girls usually wear white dresses and veils – as if they were brides – to attend their First Communion.

First Communion

When Roman Catholic children are about eight years old, they take First Communion. They join in the Mass (see page 19) by eating the bread, and sometimes also drinking the wine, which they believe becomes Jesus' body and blood. It is a very important moment for them and their parents.

(see page 19)

What is confirmation?

During this ceremony, a person 'confirms' the promises of faith that their parents made for them when they were baptized. They kneel before the bishop, he places his hands on their head and they promise to be faithful to God for the rest of their lives. Confirmation usually happens after the age of 11, once the person has started to study Christianity.

Marriage

When Christian couples marry, they come to church to make promises before God to care for and love each other whatever happens. To seal their promises, the bridegroom traditionally places a ring on his bride's finger. Nowadays, the couple might both exchange rings.

▶ At an Orthodox wedding service, crowns are held above the heads of the bride and groom because they will be 'king and queen' of their new home.

23

Holy places

There are places that are special for Christians all over the world. Many of them are in present-day Israel, the land of Jesus' birth. People visit the towns where he lived and taught, and Jerusalem where he died. **Pilgrims** come to these holy places to express their faith and, in some cases, to hope for healing.

Lourdes

In 1858, a 14-year old called Bernadette Soubirous claimed that Jesus' mother Mary appeared in front of her in Lourdes, France. Today, she is known as St. Bernadette and sick people come from all over the world to visit Lourdes believing that their illness might be cured. Not all Christians believe in the miracle of Lourdes.

◄ Many Roman Catholics make a pilgrimage to the grotto in Lourdes, France, where St. Bernadette is said to have seen the Virgin Mary.

Rome

In the heart of Rome, Italy, is the Vatican City, home to the Pope. Vast crowds gather in St. Peter's Square each Sunday to hear the Pope's message to the faithful. Roman Catholics believe that the remains of St. Peter, the founder of the Catholic Church (see page 8), lie in the Church of St. Peter.

▲ The Sea of Galilee looks calm but fierce storms can come up quickly. The Bible tells how Jesus saved the disciples' lives one night, by calming a storm when they were out together in a boat.

◄ At Easter, Christians come to Jerusalem to remember the last week of Jesus' life. On Good Friday pilgrims carrying crosses follow the route that Jesus took on the way to his crucifixion (see page 7).

Where is Galilee?

Galilee, a town in the north of present-day Israel, was the place where Jesus did much of his teaching. It is beside the Sea of Galilee, a lake that is rich in fish. Jesus' disciples came from Galilee and some of them, including Peter and John, were fishermen.

Jerusalem

Jerusalem is where Jesus was crucified and where, the Bible says, he rose from the dead. When Jesus arrived in Jerusalem he rode on a donkey to show that he was not a military King. Christians remember that day on Palm Sunday, a week before Easter Day.

Festivals and traditions

Christians celebrate events in the life of Jesus and the most important Christian festival is Easter. Christians believe that this is the time when Jesus rose from the dead (see page 7). Some Christians also remember the lives of the saints and of Mary, the mother of Jesus. Mary is especially important to Roman Catholics and to Orthodox Christians.

▼ Presents are given at Christmas to remember gifts brought to the baby Jesus by the wise men.

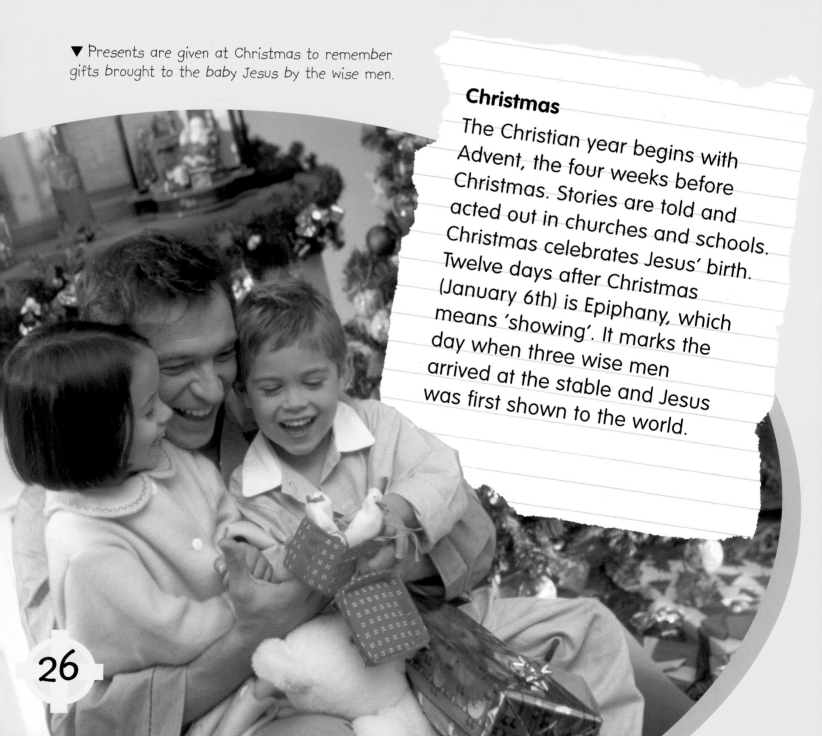

Christmas

The Christian year begins with Advent, the four weeks before Christmas. Stories are told and acted out in churches and schools. Christmas celebrates Jesus' birth. Twelve days after Christmas (January 6th) is Epiphany, which means 'showing'. It marks the day when three wise men arrived at the stable and Jesus was first shown to the world.

Easter

Easter is both a happy and a sad time. Jesus was crucified on Good Friday, and on this day Christians remember his pain. Two days later, on Easter Day, Christians rejoice that Jesus rose from the dead. There are services of celebration in church and Easter eggs are eaten to symbolize the 'new life' in Christ.

▲ Torches and candles are lit on Easter Day to celebrate the risen Christ.

Shrove Tuesday

For 40 days before Easter, Christians give up their favourite food to remember the days that Jesus spent starving in the desert before his arrest. This is called Lent. On Shrove Tuesday, the day before Lent starts, people make pancakes. Originally, pancakes were made to use up all the butter and eggs before the fasting started.

Make pancakes

You will need: 50g plain flour • pinch of salt • mixing bowl • 1 egg • 100ml milk mixed with 35ml water • whisk • butter • frying pan • plate • lemon • maple syrup, honey or sugar

1 Put the flour and salt in a mixing bowl. Make a hollow in the centre and break the egg into it. Add the liquid slowly and mix with the spoon until you have a smooth batter. Then add one tablespoon of melted butter.

2 Melt a little butter in the pan and swirl it around. Tip the egg and flour mixture in and tilt the pan so that the batter covers the base. After half a minute or so, the pancake should be cooked on the underside.

3 Ask an adult to help you toss the pancake and catch it on the uncooked side. After a few seconds, put it on a plate and serve with a squeeze of lemon and syrup, honey or sugar. Now make more!

27

Activities

Make a tree of happiness

You will need: pencil • different-coloured card • scissors • small tree branch • old newspaper • gold or silver spray paint • bucket • sand • cotton thread • material or wrapping paper

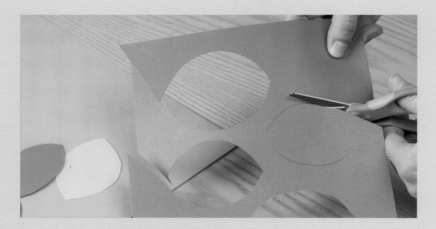

1 Draw leaf shapes on the card and cut them out. With a pencil, make a hole in the tip of each leaf. Then put the tree branch on old newspaper outdoors and ask an adult to spray it all over with gold or silver paint.

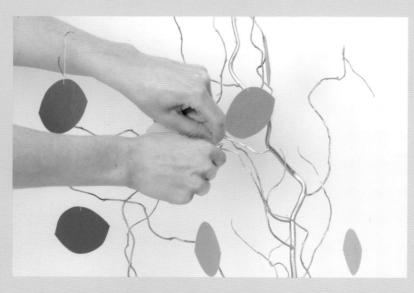

2 Fill a bucket with sand. Once the branch is dry, stand it up in the middle of the bucket. Feed thread through the hole on each leaf. Every time something good happens to your family, hang a leaf on the tree.

3 You could cover the bucket with pretty material or wrapping paper. Why not write messages on the leaf cards before you hang them up? Or make some extra leaf cards so that your friends can add their happy thoughts, too.

Make a stained-glass window

You will need: A4 black card • white crayon • craft knife
• different-coloured tissue paper • glue • sticky tape

1 Decide on a design for your stained-glass window. You might want to practise drawing it in rough first. Once you are happy with your design, draw it onto a piece of black card or paper using a white crayon.

2 Ask an adult to cut out your design with a craft knife. Then turn the card over.

3 Cut out different-coloured pieces of tissue paper. Each piece needs to be bigger than the hole it will cover. Put glue around the edge of each hole, press on the tissue paper and trim away any excess.

4 Once your stained-glass window is completely dry, use sticky tape to fix it to a real window. The sunlight will shine through the tissue paper and make the colours glow.

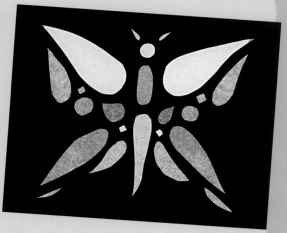

▲ This window shows Jesus as the Good Shepherd caring for his sheep, while the Holy Spirit (the dove) watches over him.

Church windows

Look at stained-glass windows in local churches. They often show pictures of Jesus, or events in his life or the lives of the saints. Sometimes they just have panels of beautiful colours.

29

Glossary

altar A holy table at the front of a church, usually covered with a cloth.

Anglicans Members of the Church of England, the Church of Ireland, the Church in Wales, the Espiscopal Church in Scotland or the Episcopal Church in the United States.

baptism Sprinkling water onto a person's forehead, or immersing them in water, to show that they are joining the Christian Church.

blasphemy Disrespectful talk about God or sacred things.

cathedral The most important church in a region, containing the bishop's throne.

Creation An event described in the Bible when God created the Universe.

crucified Put to death by being nailed or tied to a wooden cross.

disciple One of Jesus' first 12 followers.

Evangelical Christians who feel that God speaks directly to them through the Bible, not through the Pope or bishops.

Last Supper The last meal Jesus shared with his disciples before his death. He broke bread and drank wine, asking them to remember him whenever they ate bread and drank wine.

leprosy An infectious disease that causes disfigurement.

miracle An extraordinary event that cannot be explained by nature or science.

monk A man who has joined a religious order and promised to live a simple, unmarried life.

Nobel Peace Prize A prize given each year to the person who has done the most to promote world peace.

nun A woman who has joined a religious order and promised to live a simple, unmarried life.

outcast A person who is rejected by society and shunned or ignored by everyone.

persecute To treat someone badly, sometimes killing or imprisoning them for their beliefs.

pilgrim Someone who makes a journey to a holy place for religious reasons.

Pope The Bishop of Rome, the leader of the Roman Catholic Church.

resurrection An event described in the Bible when Jesus returned from the dead.

sect A group of people who share the same beliefs.

sermon A religious talk.

sin Something which goes against God's wishes, as they were described in the Bible.

symbolize When an object or event is used to suggest something else.

wafer A thin circular piece of bread eaten at Mass.

worship To praise God.

Index

Notes for parents and teachers

This book is an accessible introduction to the beliefs and practices of the Christian faith. It does not aim to be a comprehensive guide but gives plenty of opportunity for further activities and study. The content is closely linked to the non-statutory framework for Religious Education, particularly the QCA schemes of work listed below. The topics selected also overlap with locally agreed RE syllabuses.

Unit 1A: What does it mean to belong?
Unit 1D: Beliefs and practice
Unit 2B: Why did Jesus tell stories?
Unit 2C: Celebrations
Unit 2D: Visiting a place of worship
Unit 3A: What do signs and symbols mean in religion?
Unit 4D: What religions are represented in our neighbourhood?
Unit 5C: Where did the Christian Bible come from?
Unit 6A: Worship and community
Unit 6C: Why are sacred texts important?

Visiting a church

A church or chapel tells you a great deal about Christianity. At the heart of a church's reason for being is the worship of Jesus. It is a place to read from the Bible, a place to be the centre of the community where people teach and learn about the Christian faith. Visits to churches should not be solely concerned with information but should also explore feelings and allow the senses to speak. It is helpful if the church is not empty when you visit and there is music playing. If visits are carefully chosen, children will be able to see how different churches can be, which will give them some insight into the rich diversity of Christianity.

Reading the Bible

Most Bible stories are over 2,000 years old but they explore aspects of human experience that are recognizable to us today. Read the stories with the children and encourage them to discuss the feelings of the people in the stories.

More books to read

Encounter Christianity: Key Stages 1 and 2
Alan Brown and Alison Seaman,
Church House Publishing 2001

The Bible
Alan Brown, Evans Brothers 2003

Jesus and Christianity
Alan Brown, Wayland 2002

Worship and Jesus and Mary
Alison Seaman and Graham Owen, Wayland 1998

Useful websites

www.theresite.org.uk
A good place to explore religion on the web.

www.bbc.co.uk/religion/religions/christianity
A useful site for general information on many aspects of Christianity.

www.whychristmas.com
Useful collection of Christmas ideas for all ages with information about different traditions around the world.